# This book is presented to:

_____

## From:

_____

## Date:

_____

# Happy Birthday to Me

## Written by David and Tessie DeVore

## Illustration by

## Heather Graham

Charisma
KIDS
A STRANG COMPANY

*Happy Birthday to Me*
by David and Tessie DeVore

Requests for information may be addressed to:

The children's book imprint of Strang Communications Company
600 Rinehart Rd., Lake Mary, FL 32746
www.charismakids.com

Children's Editor: Gwen Ellis
Text by Trisha Throop
Copyeditor: Jevon Oakman Bolden
Design Director: Mark Poulalion
Designed by Joe De Leon

Library of Congress Control Number 2004101614
International Standard Book Number 1-59185-207-2

05 06 07 08 09 — 98765432
Printed in China

In memory of our Mami Esther and Abuela Mita whose love for family and faith in God inspired this story.

To our family/familia, especially our parents: Francisco Güell, William and Kay DeVore, who taught us the value of God, family, and love.

—David and Tessie DeVore

Today is my birthday! I am awake early. I can't wait to see my whole family. I get to open my birthday presents. Then we'll eat my birthday cake!

My name is David Alejandro, and this is my *Mami* (Mommy).

She gives me a big hug and says, "Happy birthday to you, David.
I remember the day God gave you to us. It was a wonderful day!"

I smile a big smile. "Where's *Papi* (Daddy)?"

"He's out in the backyard, and he needs your help,"
*Mami* tells me.

When I get outside, I see *Papi* holding a bright purple and yellow *piñata*.

"Happy birthday to you David!" he says.

"Thank you, *Papi*. Can I help?"

"Yes, you may," *Papi* tells me, and he hands me the long rope on the *piñata*.

I pull down on the rope so the *piñata* swings up in the air. The *piñata* is heavy, because it is full of candy.

*Papi* ties the rope so the *piñata* won't fall.

"Ding-dong, ding-dong!" We hear the doorbell ring.

"Who is it?" I ask and then open the door for my four grandparents. My Grandpa and Grandma have always lived in the United States. My *Abuela* and *Abuelo* came from Puerto Rico.

"Hi, Grandma and Grandpa," I say in English.

"*Hola, Abuela y Abuelo*," I say in Spanish.

"Happy birthday to you, David!" they smile and cheer.

"David, you are a gift from God!" Grandma says and smiles.

"Yes, God gave us all a gift, and it was you. Now we want to give you gifts on your special day," laughs *Abuelo*.

Soon the rest of my family and friends arrive at our house. *Papi* looks at me and says, "David, let's start the party."

My friends and cousins and I run outside to play Pin the Tail on the Donkey.

When we finish that game,
we are ready for the *piñata*
game. We wear blindfolds and
take turns trying to break
the *piñata* with sticks. Finally
my cousin hits the *piñata*
as hard as he can. It
breaks. Down comes
a shower of candy.
Grandma and *Abuela*
watch and laugh
as the candy falls on
everyone.

"David is so blessed to be part of two cultures on his special day," says Grandma.

"Yes, we celebrate birthdays in different ways, but we are all the same family!" says *Abuela*.

When the games are done, *Papi* calls, "Is anyone hungry?"

Some of us say, "Yes! Yes! Let's eat!"
The rest of us say, "*Sí, vamos a comer.*"

Before we eat, Grandpa calls everyone together.

"It's time for a special family blessing!" he says.

Grandpa and *Abuelo* pray: "Father, we thank You for David Alejandro. Thank You for the way You brought two cultures together in him. Bless David and help our families show others that we are stronger when we embrace our differences. Thank You for a wonderful day. Amen!"

After we eat, we sing: "Happy Birthday" and "*Feliz Cumpleaños.*" I blow out the candles. "Happy birthday to me!"

Happy Birthday · Feliz cumpleaños

GUAYABERA / SHIRT

CAMISA / T-SHIRT

Dios tiene un plan para ti

VIDEO / VÍDEO

BOLA DE FÚTBOL / SOCCER BALL

BOLA DE FÚTBOL AMERICANO / FOOTBALL

Un corazón para Jesús

Discovery Cove

LIBRO / BOOK

I open presents next! I got a football and a soccer ball. I got a T-shirt and a special shirt called a *guayabera*. I also got books and movies in Spanish and English.

"Thank you very much! *Gracias*!" I say to everyone. "This is the best birthday ever!"

"Here are some of the foods we ate at my party."

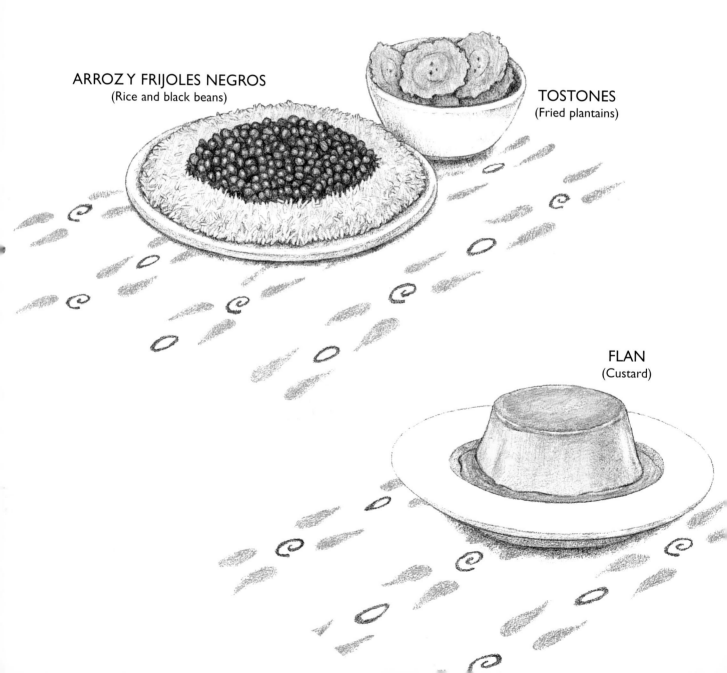

ARROZ Y FRIJOLES NEGROS
(Rice and black beans)

TOSTONES
(Fried plantains)

FLAN
(Custard)

**HAMBURGUESA CON
QUESO Y PAPAS FRITAS**
(Cheeseburger and fries)

**HABICHUELAS TIERNAS**
(Green beans)

# Note to Parents

The population of the United States is more diverse than ever before!
In the last decade alone, the Hispanic population has swelled 58 percent.
The composition of the Hispanic population is also undergoing fundamental
changes. According to the Pew Hispanic Center, births to Hispanic couples
in the United States are outpacing immigration as the key source of growth.
Over the next twenty years this will produce an important shift in the
makeup of the Hispanic population with second-generation Latinos. Children
born to immigrant parents will emerge as the largest component of that
population. Many of these children will be the result of Latinos marrying
non-Latinos.

We are one of those families. One day, when we asked our son what he
wanted for dinner, he responded: "I want *pollo* (chicken), French fries,
*pan* (bread), and sweet tea." We laughed as we realized that this is his
life—a life merging the best of two worlds. We also understood that God
has plans for our son, and He has plans for all the children of multi-ethnic
homes. Think about it! These children will be able to walk in and out of two
cultures and feel at ease in either one. These children will grow up speak-
ing more than one language and will be able to share the love of Jesus with
more people than any previous generation!

Whatever your cultural background, we encourage you to instill in your
children a love for all nations, ethnic groups, races, and languages. If you are
like us, in doing so you will be teaching them to love all that makes them
who they are: everything that God will one day use for His glory.

The Bible tells us in Revelation 7:9 that one day people from all walks of life
will stand before the Lord. "A great multitude that no one could count, from
every nation, tribe, people, and language, standing before the throne and in
front of the Lamb."

—David and Tessie DeVore